DON'T SEND YOURSELF TO HELL

BETTY WOOLEY

WESTBOW
PRESS®
A DIVISION OF THOMAS NELSON
& ZONDERVAN

This book is a work of non-fiction. Unless otherwise noted, the author
and the publisher make no explicit guarantees as to the accuracy of
the information contained in this book and in some cases, names of
people and places have been altered to protect their privacy.

WestBow Press books may be ordered through booksellers or by contacting:

WestBow Press
A Division of Thomas Nelson & Zondervan
1663 Liberty Drive
Bloomington, IN 47403
www.westbowpress.com
844-714-3454

Because of the dynamic nature of the Internet, any web addresses or
links contained in this book may have changed since publication and
may no longer be valid. The views expressed in this work are solely those
of the author and do not necessarily reflect the views of the publisher,
and the publisher hereby disclaims any responsibility for them.

Any people depicted in stock imagery provided by Getty Images are
models, and such images are being used for illustrative purposes only.
Certain stock imagery © Getty Images.

ISBN: 978-1-6642-8301-5 (sc)
ISBN: 978-1-6642-8302-2 (e)

Library of Congress Control Number: 2022920281

Print information available on the last page.

WestBow Press rev. date: 01/09/2023

ABOUT THE AUTHOR

Betty Wooley is a 91-year-old mother to seven children, a registered nurse since 1952 and a practicing Christian since she was a child. She taught about missions in her church and has been on several mission trips to other countries.

She was working in a busy emergency room until December of 2007 when she was forced to retire after an illness. She was 76 and had worked as a registered nurse for over 50 years.

She wants you to know that life is uncertain and some people will be going to their eternity sooner than planned. She knows that a 91 year old will perhaps think about dying more than a 21 year old, it is a good thing to think about dying while there is still time.

She also wants you to know that God does not send anyone to hell-- He wants every one to turn from their sins and accept Jesus as their savior. If you do that you can plan on spending your eternity in Heaven------ otherwise you will be going to hell.

Don't send yourself to hell.

PREFACE

Would you want someone living in your house who didn't love you? Would you want someone living in your house who might steal from you! Someone you couldn't trust. Neither does God. God cannot look upon sin. Sin will not be permitted in Heaven.

Even if we cannot read or write, the Bible tells us we know right from wrong. If you are a practicing homosexual, you know in your heart you are sinning and any amount of protesting, marching or legislation will not negate God's laws. God calls this an abomination and your doom will be in the Lake that burns with fire and sulfur. Another sin that society seems to be accepting as normal is a man and woman living together without benefit of marriage. This is fornication. Sinful relationships will send you to Hell for your eternity.

Here is a partial list of sins found in the Bible:

- Idol worshipers
- Adultery
- Wanting what belongs to others
- Wickedness

- Deceit
- Lewdness
- Envy
- Slander
- Pride
- Those conversing with demons
- Murderers
- He who justifies the wicked
- He who condemns the good
- Evil actions
- Lust
- Practicing homosexuality Fornication
- Drunkenness
- Liars
- Greedy people
- Sexual Sins: No other sin affects the body as this does because you sin against your own body. And our body belongs to Jesus Christ. Jesus died on a cross to pay for the sins of those who love Him and have accepted them or their sorrow.
- The Immoral - Those who lead immoral lives
- The corrupt
- Those who are unfaithful to God!
- Cowards who won't follow Jesus
- Robbers
- Demon worshipers
- Those who lead immoral lives

If you find yourself on this list, you might need to run to get your name in the Lamb's Book of Life just in case you should die suddenly and find yourself in Hell.

Those who lead immoral lives, idol worshipers, greedy people, drunkards, slanderers or those practicing homosexuality or fornication will be sent to the lake that burns with fire and sulfur. Some sins today are so common, people may think its normal in today's world. The word of God tells us, if an individual is practicing homosexual, it's an abomination and they are doomed to the Lake of Fire that burns with fire and sulfur.

Does God love you if you are a practicing homosexual? Yes - God loves you as much as He loves me and I have been a Christian for eighty (80) years. The difference is, I will spend my eternity in Heaven with Jesus.

If you die without accepting Christ as your Savior, you will spend an eternity in Hell. You must be "born again" to spend eternity with Jesus in Heaven. You ask what you need to do. First of all, you need to admit you are a sinner and since we are all sinners, that shouldn't be too hard to admit. You need to be sorry for your sins and be willing to repent. Jesus Christ came to this earth to save us from our sins by dying on a cross for us. He loves us. He wants us in Heaven with Him for eternity. Now, if you accept

Jesus as your Savior and you are sorry for your sins, you can call yourself a Christian because you have been "born again". God will punish sin wherever it is found Romans: 2: 12-16.

INTRODUCTION

Are you a practicing homosexual - by the way, man's laws do not negate God's laws. God calls this an abomination and unless you are sorry for this, you will be thrown in the Lake that burns with fire and sulfur when you die. Are you living with someone without benefit of marriage. This is immoral and unless you are sorry for this, you will be thrown in the Lake that burns with fire and sulfur.

Do you steal or lie or want what belongs to others? Any sin is forgivable but "one" and that is the sin of rejecting Jesus.

God loves us, He made us. He wants us to live with Him in Heaven for eternity. I love you too! I may have taken care of you in the emergency room. You may have come from jail, where you were in a fight, battered and bruised or you came with your children because you were cold and homeless. I loved you all, but Jesus loves you more. He hung on a cross and died to pay for our sins - so that if we are sorry for our sins and accept Jesus as our Savior, we can live with Him forever because our eternity will be with Him in Heaven.

Life is uncertain - like the oil field worker who was "dead on arrival" at the Emergency Room one morning when I went to work. When he put his boots on that day, he never knew that this would be his last day on earth. I pray that he had prepared for his eternity and belonged to Jesus.

If you are ready to admit you are a sinner and want to accept Jesus and live forever with Him in Heaven for an eternity, you might pray a prayer something like this: "Dear Lord, I know I am a sinner and I am sorry. I want Jesus to come into my heart and be my Savior". If you pray this prayer and are sincere, you now belong to Jesus and you will be with Him forever in Heaven when you die. NOTE: Not all people who call themselves Christians are really Christians!

He is merciful and tender toward those who sinners and Christians alike. But only those who are sorry for their sins and have accepted Jesus as their Savior will get to go to Heaven when they die, and it's a good thing to think about dying while there is still time. Eccl 7:2 We must account to God for everything we do. We are to fear God and obey His commandments for that is the entire duty of man. BUT more about God! He forgives all our sins (if we are sorry). He heals me.

He ransoms me with loving kindness and tender mercies.

He fills my life with good things.

He gives justice to all who are treated unfairly. He is merciful and tender toward those who love him.

ACKNOWLEDGEMENTS

JESUS   Thank you, thank you for dying on a cross to pay for my sins so that I might spend my eternity with you in Heaven.

MOTHER   Thank you for being a Christian mother who taught me about Jesus with words and deeds.

SON   Thank you for being such a good son in helping me with this book and working with the publishing. Thank you for reading my book and checking to make sure Jesus would agree with my thoughts

HELL

A place for those who are not sorry for their sins and have not accepted Jesus as their Savior. This would be for an eternity in Hell!

DON'T CALL EVIL GOOD

INDEX

1. HELL
A place for those who are not sorry for their sins and have not accepted Jesus as their Savior. This would be for an eternity in Hell!

2. DON'T CALL EVIL GOOD
Don't say that right is wrong and what is wrong is right.

3. THE SIN OF BEING SILENT
Whoever knows the right thing to do - but doesn't do it - for them it is a sin. Anything that is not God's will.

4. LOVE AND GOD
About Love - God is love. God - our creator

5. SIN
Sins and definitions mentioned in the Bible

6. ABOUT HEAVEN
A place for those who are sorry for their sins and love Jesus will spend their eternity

Ezekiel 3:18-19

Isaiah 58:6

James 4:17

HELL

W e are all going to spend an eternity somewhere and there are only two places available. That is Heaven or Hell. It will be your decision because if you choose Heaven, you have to admit you are a sinner and you want to turn from your sins and accept Jesus Christ as your Savior. If you don't choose Heaven that only leaves Hell and if you choose Hell, you don't have to do anything. You can be a very bad person or a very good person. If you haven't chosen Jesus, you are going to Hell. It is your choice.

If you choose Hell, you will be thrown into a fiery furnace where the fire never goes out and there will be weeping and gnashing of teeth. The smoke of their torment goes up forever. They will have no rest day or night.

Jesus said at the end of the world, the angels will come and separate the wicked people from the godly. The godly are the people who have turned from their sins and accepted Jesus as their Savior, casting the wicked (people who have not accepted Jesus as their Savior) into the fire. The Bible describes Hell as a fiery inferno and a place of torment. The Bible says many will be cast into outer darkness into the place of weeping and torment. Hell is also described as a place of eternal punishment and a place of eternal fire prepared for the devil and his angels. Hell is also described as a fiery furnace and if

BETTY WOOLEY

your name is not written in the book of life he will be thrown in the lake of fire. It is also described as a blazing furnace, fire of hell, eternal fire, unquenchable fire and tormented with fire and brimstone.

Hell is a place of darkness, weeping, torment, anguish, and the place of everlasting fire. the bible says that the cowardly, the faithless, the detestable, murderers, the sexually immoral, sorcerers, idolaters, and all liars will be in the lake of fire.

Just another reminder that we send ourselves to hell by rejecting Jesus. I find it easy to love someone who loves me so much that he died qi the cross to pay for my sins, if I truly love Him. Of course, He arose and after three days He was soon again on this earth. Jesus mentioned Hell more times in the Bible than Heaven. He paid a price of dying on the cross so that anyone who loves and believes in Him should have everlasting life in Heaven.

Back to what Hell is like! It is described as a furnace of fire and he will be tormented with fire and brimstone. Hell will be a place of conscious suffering, hot with no water and you will be tormented day and night forever and ever for an eternity in the unquenchable fire. Hell is also described as a furnace of fire.

Just a reminder that the wages of sin in death but God gives us a free gift of eternal life with Him, if we are sorry for our sins and accepts Jesus Christ as our

Savior. Our names are put in the Book of Life after we have accepted Jesus as our Savior and when we die, we will go to Heaven. But, if our name is not found in the Book of Life, we will be thrown in the lake of fire, and the smoke of their torment goes on forever and ever and there will be no rest day or night.

Jesus spoke about Hell more than anyone. Why? Because He loves us, He died on the cross for us and He wants you to know what Hell is like, so you can make your decision to either go to Hell or Heaven. It should be easy to accept someone who loves you over someone (the Devil) who doesn't love you and wants you with him in Hell. Jesus wants you in Heaven with Him because you love Him. He is worthy of our love and He does not want you to sin because of what sin does. It destroys homes and people - that is Satan's way - but God's way is love. That is why He was crucified on the cross to pay for our sins. Jesus says that Hell is a place of eternal torment and of unquenchable fire where the worm does not die and people will gnash their teeth in anguish and from which there is no return. He calls it a place of utter darkness, where the worm will not die. Hell is eternal. Hell is painful. Hell is a lake of fire. Hell is eternal. Hell is a place of darkness. Hell is a place of fire. There is not rest in Hell. There is no relief in Hell!

Hell is very difficult to write about. It is very painful

to think about and we all only have one life to choose where we spend eternity, so we need to read about Hell and think about Hell, so we can make a decision as to where we will spend eternity. I choose Jesus because He loves me. How do I know He loves me? We, first of all I can feel His love. I can talk to Him. He was crucified on the cross to pay for our sins. God cannot look upon sin. God shows His anger from Heaven against all sinful, evil men, for the truth about God is known to all instinctively for God has put this knowledge in their hearts.

To recap some descriptions of Hell: Realm of darkness, thrown outside into the darkness, blackest darkness, plunged into darkness, gnashing of teeth, blazing furnace, fire of Hell, eternal Hell, unquenchable fire, tormented with fire, everlasting punishment.

So now you know Hell is forever and ever and you will be in a place of darkness and pain with no rest and you will retain your mental faculties with no hope, and no relief. This is for an eternity.

No one wants to spend an eternity in Hell, and God has given you a choice. To choose Hell, you do not have to do anything. To choose Heaven, you have to admit you are a sinner. The Bible Says we have all sinned and come short of the glory of God. So it shouldn't be too hard to admit that. Then, we have to accept Jesus (God's son) into our hearts to be our Savior. Jesus loves us. He died on the cross to pay for our sins. We owed a debt we could not pay and He paid a debt He did not owe. With a love like that, how could you not love Jesus? You do all that and now you are a Christian. You belong to God and nothing can separate you. You're going to try very hard not to sin and when you do slip and sin, you'll be sorry and if you ask for forgiveness from your sin, God is quick to forgive you. You have to be really sorry though. You can't pretend. God knows the difference.

After you belong to God, you will want to tell your relatives, friends and others how to accept Jesus as their Lord. and Savior and live with him in Heaven (God's house). We are not promised tomorrow so the time to tell others how to live in Heaven forever is now. After we have accepted Christ as our Savior, we must tell others to think that anyone should spend an eternity in Hell is so painful, but God has showed us how to spend eternity with Him in Heaven.

God is love and He wants you to spend eternity with Him. He does not want you in Hell. God forgives your sin if you only ask. For God loved the world so much that He gave His only son that whoever believes in Him will not perish (go to Hell) but have everlasting eternal life with Him in Heaven. Jesus died for our sins. Now that is love!

Now that you have accepted Jesus as your Savior, it

is time to tell others how to have an eternity in Heaven after we die.

Remember, that God will forgive any sin if you are sorry for doing it. the only sin God will not forgive is blasphemy against the Holy Spirit.

THE SIN OF
BEING SILENT

As Christians, we are to tell the lost about God's plan for the lost to accept Jesus as their Savior and how to live with Jesus forever and ever in God's house (Heaven).

There is sin in being silent. If we see someone who is continuing in sin, we must gently and kindly tell them that they must turn from their sin and turn to God so they can be forever with Jesus. If we say to the wicked that you shall surely die and how do we tell someone who is living with another person without the benefit of marriage that unless they repent and turn to Jesus they will not be entitled to heaven live forever with Jesus in gods house. Tell them what the bible says. The bible is the inspired word of God. How do we tell a practicing homosexual that he will not go to heaven unless he says sorry for their sins and repents and turn to Jesus. We must tell them what the bible says that unless they repent and turn to Jesus they will not be awarded a place in Gods house. (Heaven) To live with Jesus forever the bible which is the inspired word of God it has all the rules for us to go by. We can not ignore sin or pretend that it is okay that would be winking at sin and it seems millions of people are "winking at sin" and those who are winking at sin will be held accountable. Are you living together without benefit of marriage? That is fornication and if you died without repenting what about your eternity in heaven or what about your eternity in hell. Eternity is forever and once you die you will not be able to make any changes. That is why now is the time to repent of your sins and accept Jesus as your savior. Why? Because Jesus loves us. He died on the cross for our sins. Why? Because Jesus loves us. He created us and our God is a zealous God. Because he created us and died for our sins to provide a way for us to spend an eternity with him we are assured an eternity in heaven with Jesus if we accept him as our savior after we are sorry for our sins. Life on this earth is short and after our life on this earth is over when what? We die and we either go to heaven or hell for our eternity. Now to spend an eternity in hell we do not have to do anything. To spend an eternity in heaven we have to admit we are sinners and are sorry for our sins and we want to accept Jesus as our savior. Then we will try very hard not to sin and when we do we will be very sorry for our sins. God created us. He wants the best for us. That is why He gave us rules and commandments to go by. He knows we will make mistakes and as Christians, we will be sorry for our mistakes and God is quick to forgive us! Why? Because God is our Heavenly Father and He wants to spend an eternity with us. He also wants us to tell others how to spend an eternity in Heaven with Him. So you see we cannot be silent about sin. Sin is sin, evil is evil, and is not good. To continue sinning in an unrepentant manner leads to death physically, emotionally and spiritual death. If our best friend is living with someone without benefit of marriage, they are sinning. If you have friends who are practicing homosexuality, they are sinning. If you have a friend who is stealing, they are also sinning. We cannot look the other way. They are sinning. Do you want them to know that these and other sins lead straight to Hell. You must tell them what the Bible says about these sins. We must tell people about the plan of salvation to live in Heaven for an eternity. Don't wink at sin when where you spend eternity is the most important decision you will ever make. Jesus wants us all in Heaven with Him but the choice is ours. Do we choose Heaven or Hell. If we choose Heaven, we have to go by God's rules. To choose Hell, we simply have to do nothing. God's rules to get into Heaven are, first, we have to admit we are sinners, we have to be sorry for our sins and want to stop sinning. We will want to accept Jesus as our Savior and go by His rules. The road to Heaven is narrow and the road to Hell is wide but the road to Heaven leads to an eternity with Jesus in God's house, while the road to Hell leads to burning forever, separated forever from our loved ones. Forever is a long time. It goes on and on, never ending. God loves us and wants us to spend our eternity with Him in the perfect home He is building, which is called Heaven, where there is no pain or sorrow. If we believe in Jesus and accept Him as our Savior. He has paid for our sins. He is our way to Heaven. He loves us so much. He died on the cross to pay for our sins. We owed a debt we could not pay. Jesus paid a debt He did not owe and if you are in Christ, you will be with Him forever, so resist evil and depend on the Lord to fight it.

DON'T CALL
EVIL GOOD

T he Lord despises those who say that bad is good and good is bad and he who justifies the wicked and he who condemns the righteous. Both of them, alike, are an abomination to the Lord. The Bible says winking at sin leads to sorrow and bold proof leads to peace. There are a lot of sins in this world today and some of those sins that society is winking at is homosexuality. The Bible is very plain about this sin, here are some: One: If a man has sexual relations with a man as one does with a woman both of them have done what is detestable. They are to be put to death. Their blood will be on their own heads. Do you not know that wrongdoers will not inherit the Kingdom of God? Do not be deceived. Neither the sexually immoral nor idolaters nor adulterers nor men who have sex with men nor thieves nor the greedy nor drunkards nor slanderers will inherit the Kingdom of God. People who practice homosexuality know they are sinning. They do not need for people to wink at their sin and say that bad is good. We want our friends, loved ones and others we know, to spend an eternity with Jesus in Heaven. They must be told of God's love for them. For God so loved the world that He gave His only son so that anyone who believes in Him, shall not perish but have everlasting life. Practicing homosexuality is a sin. One that will take you on the wide path to Hell. Practicing homosexuality would not be worth spending an eternity in Hell. God loves you. If you're sorry for this sin and ask God to forgive you, He is quick to forgive. Two: Another sin that society is winking at is fornication. This is sex between an unmarried man and woman. In this year of 2021, it has become quite common. If you are living together without being married or having sex without being married, you are in danger of spending an eternity in Hell. Actually let me rephrase that, scripture makes it clear that fornicators will not inherit the Kingdom of God. That leaves only Hell and Hell will be for an eternity of fire and brimstone. God will forgive you of this sin if you are truly sorry.

Three: Abortion is another sin that some in society condone. God said, "Before I formed you in the womb, I knew you, before you were born, I set you apart". If God set us apart before we were born and if He knew us before we were conceived, would it not be murder if that child was aborted? The Bible says, but cowards who turn back from following me, and the corrupt and murderers and the immoral and those conversing with demons and idol worshipers and all liars their doom is in the lake that burns with fire and sulfur. Don't have an abortion.

We are now hearing a lot about gender. God said 'let us make man in our own image'. So God created man in his own image, in the image of God by Him; male and female created Him. That shouldn't be to hard to understand. He made male and female. But from the beginning of creation God made them male and female - now that I know you can understand. These sins that I have just written about are sins that are plaguing our society today. Homosexuality, fornication are sins that if practiced, the person will be going to Hell. These are God's rules. It is His house in Heaven and He is very careful as to who gets invited to live in it forever. It is your choice. Don't send yourself to Hell. Would you want someone living in your house that didn't love you? Someone that might steal from you, someone you couldn't trust, someone who wouldn't go by your rules?

Neither does Jesus. But once you get to know Him and to love Him, you will want to follow His rules. You would try very hard to be someone HE would want at his home. If you don't know Him, I can introduce you - His name is Jesus and He is the son of God. He already knows you; actually, He knows how many hairs you have on your head. He already loves you (because God is love).

He insists on His children loving each other.

We have to follow God's rules or we don't get invited into his House. If you love God and break a rule and are truly sorry and ask to be forgiven, God is quick to forgive. Some of His rules are hard to follow. He has given them to us in a book called the Bible. Which is a book he inspired several people to write. People who loved Him. It is an old book probably about 2700 years ago and, I guess you could say, it has directions for living our lives as God wants us to. Oh, it also has a lot of history, actually since the beginning of the world. Some of the names of the people are very hard to pronounce.

The Bible has been around all these years even though some people (who didn't like it) tried to get rid of it. It has all the rules in it. It is hard to read and understand in some places but it will be worth it. Because, if you get to know Jesus and want Him to be your Savior, you will be invited some day to His house. Quite frankly, if you are not invited to His house, the only other place for you to go is Hell! Jesus has a very strict rule about getting into His house. He said, "unless you are born again, you cannot get into my house" (which is the Kingdom of God). Jesus said anyone who believe in me will have eternal life. eternal life is forever and ever living in God's house. For God so loved the world that He gave His only son so that anyone who believes in Him shall not perish but have eternal life.

SIN

One definition of sin is that it is an offense against religion or moral law. However, we do not need to lookup any definition of sin because the Bible tells us that God will punish the heathen when they sin even through they have never had God's written laws for down in their hearts, they know right from wrong. So even though we all know when we do wrong (sin), I am going to list some sins that are listed in the Bible because sin separates us from God. The Bible says that we have all sinned so what can we do. The Bible also says that Jesus died on the cross. He died to pay our debt. He died on the cross between two thieves. This is history; George Washington was America's first president. This is history and I believed it happened.

Okay, we all know when we do wrong and even so, I am going to list some of the sins mentioned in the Bible. I know that some of you are not going to like this, but because I am a Christian who loves God this must be said. I was very sorry for my past sins and asked Jesus into my heart to be my Savior. I know my sins are forgiven. Remember that Jesus died on the cross for us. He paid our debt. If that doesn't explain this. I go in to pay a ticket the person in charge tells me I don't owe anything that someone else has paid it for me.

Here is a list of some of the sins and definitions mentioned in the Bible. The penalty for homosexual acts is death to both parties. Homosexuality is absolutely forbidden for it is an enormous sin. Fornication is sexual intercourse between people not married to each other. Adultery is a consensual sexual relation between someone who is married and a person they are not married to who may or may not be married to someone else. Idolatry - an idol is anything that replaces the one true God. Some examples of idolatry is greed, hate, envy, murder, fighting, lying, bitterness, gossiping, backbiting, haters of God. So those who live immoral lives will have no share of His kingdom. That means you will not get invited to Heaven. The only other place is to go to Hell. But the choice is ours because when God created us, He gave us free will and eternal life is forever and I want to live it in God's house. For God so loved the world that He gave His only begotten son that who ever believes in Him should not perish but have everlasting life.

God will punish sin wherever it is found. He will punish the heathen even though they never had God's written laws for down in their hearts, they know right from wrong. So the most important decision we will ever make is confessing that we are sinners and accepting Jesus Christ as our Savior. Remember, Her died on the cross to pay for our sins. Now that is love, Jesus loves us so much, God is love. But the wages of sin is death but the free gift of God is eternal life through Jesus Christ, our Lord. Don't send yourself to Hell. Come to Jesus and confess your sins. Be sorry for doing them. Ask Jesus to come into your heart and be your Savior, it is that simple. Jesus loves you and wants you to live with Him forever in His home that is called Heaven This chapter on sin is so important for you to know that sin separates us from God. The Bible says that wrongdoers will not inherit the Kingdom of God which means wrongdoers will not be invited to God's house (Heaven). It also says, do not be deceived, heathen, the sexually immoral or idolaters, nor thieves, nor the greedy, nor the drunkards, nor slanderers will inherit the Kingdom of God. But if we confess our sins, He is faithful and just and will forgive our sins. There is only one sin that is unforgivable and that is blasphemy against the Holy Spirit. If we reject Jesus, we will not get invited to live in Heaven when we die and the only other place is Hell.

I remember going to work one morning in the emergency room, probably about 50 years ago as an emergency room Registered Nurse. I have many memories of tragedy but in one room there was a younger man lying on the bed covered with a sheet except for his boots, they were not covered.. I remember this because I'm sure as he was going to work. He never probably felt this would be the last day of his life. But had he prepared for his death by giving his heart to Jesus? Please, the most important decision you will ever make is to accept Jesus Christ as your

Savior. He loves you, remember I told you He died on the cross to pay for the sins of people who are sorry they sinned and have accepted Jesus as their Savior. He paid a debt He did not owe and we owed a debt we could not pay. What a wonderful love God has for us - red, yellow, black or white, we are all precious in His sight. He loves us all for God is love. The choice is ours to make. Do we choose a friend who loves us so much He died on the cross between two thieves. Of course, He arose from the dead and was now seen on earth afterwards. This is a matter of history. Remember, I told you the Bible has a lot of history in it. The choice is ours to be sorry for our sins and to ask Jesus to be our Savior and only then will we be promised an invitation to live with Jesus in His house forever when we die. It is a choice that if you don't make, you are sending yourself to Hell when you die. Remember the Bible says that He Himself bore our sins in His body on the cross so that we might die to sin and live for righteousness. By His wounds you have been healed. That is love and remember the only sin God will not forgive is rejecting Him.

How do you send yourself to Hell? By doing nothing, or you can prepare yourself now for an invitation to live in God's house forever. We all sin and we all know what sin is even if you have never read the Bible. If no one has ever told you how to live forever with Jesus, let me tell you. We have to be sorry for our sins and ask Jesus to come into our hearts and be our Savior.

That is very simple but let me tell you it is the best decision you will ever make. You are now a child of God and He loves you. He died on the cross to pay for our sins. Accepting Jesus as your Savior doesn't mean we will never sin again even though we will try harder to not sin, but if we do sin and are truly sorry, God is going to be quick to forgive you because He loves you and you are His child. He is our heavenly father. Some earthly fathers are not loving and some are mean and uncaring but our heavenly father loves us so much that He sent His only begotten son that whosoever believeth in Him should not perish (go to Hell) but have everlasting life. He sent His son to live on this earth and to die on a cross for our sins. No one loves us as much as God loves us. But the decision is yours to make. An eternity in God's house or an eternity in Hell!

ABOUT HEAVEN

Jesus said that He is the one who raises the dead and gives life again to anyone who believes in Him and trusts in Him to be their Savior. He said that even though He died, He will live again. He is given eternal life for believing in Jesus. In Heaven, God will wipe away every tear, there will be no more death and mourning or crying or pain. For now God has shown us a different way to Heaven. Not by being good enough but by being good and trying to keep His laws, but by a new way. Not really new, for the Bible told us about it long ago. Now God says He will accept and acquit us, declare us not guilty if we are sorry for our sins and ask Jesus to be our Savior. He will take us away and declare us not guilty because Jesus paid for our sins when he died on the cross. Look at it this way, just suppose you had a ticket and you went to pay it and you were told someone else already paid it. God loves us so much that he sent his only son so that whoever believes in him will not perish and have everlasting life. In short if you are sorry for your sins, and turn from them and ask Jesus to be your savior you will spend your eternity in Heaven. Again, let me tell you can talk to him and tell him you know you are a sinner. We all sin and come short of the glory of God. You have to turn from your sins and trust God as your savior and then tell people that Christ is your lord. That is the way to get invited to Heaven (God's House). It is very simple to understand but sometimes very hard to follow. You see, the devil does not want you to go to God's house, He wants you to go to Hell and burn forever. The Devil will try to make you think that some things are ok, take living together without being married. Just because everyone is doing it does not make it okay, it is a sin. You may think it's okay because everyone is doing it, or maybe a law has been passed that makes it seem okay. Like men married to men or a woman married to a woman. But God says that is an abomination. If we want to go to Heaven, we have to follow God's rules. God says that homosexuals and fornicators cannot go to His house. Adulterers, thieves, drunkards and people who covet will not have a share in His kingdom (no invitation to heaven). God loves us all but these are His rules and He gives us a choice. We will all sin, everyone does but we have to try very hard not to and when we sin and are really sorry and ask God's forgiveness God is quick to forgive because He loves us. Remember God's rules and God wants Christians to show people how to get to Heaven. In fact, because I am a Christian and one of God's children, I must tell people about Him (God) and His directions for our living. Again, I say God's rules are sometimes hard to follow and because the Devil wants us to go to His house (Hell) where you burn forever. He (the Devil) is trying to tempt us to do all these sins. Jesus does not tempt us but we know in our hearts what is right and what is wrong.

After you accept Jesus as your Savior, God's spirit will live in you to help you with your new life. The bible says you must be born again. Jesus told us before He was crucified not to be troubled and to trust in God and also to trust in Him. He told us that He is going to Heaven, (God's House), and there are many rooms there and he is going to prepare a place for us, and He will come back and take us to heaven. No one will be blind, deaf or lame in Heaven and people who could not talk will be able to talk, there will be only joy and gladness in Heaven. The Bible also tells us that Jesus will change our bodies like his own. There will be no more death or sorrow or crime or pain all that is gone forever. There's a lot we don't know about heaven (the bible tells us) that we will be able to know each other. There will be no marriage, there will be no tears or pain, we won't have bad emotions only good ones, for in Heaven there is no sorrow. We will be ourselves in heaven. After Jesus rose from the dead he told his disciples to look at his hands and feet. Jesus was who he was before he was crucified. Heaven is a place. Jesus told us that he was going to prepare a place for us. God will wipe away all our tears. There will be no more death, or sorrow or pain or crime. There are a lot of questions about heaven that are not answered in the bible but since God created this world with all its imperfections, we will love Heaven and will for all of eternity. An eternity in Heaven is your choice.

It is very simple, first we have to admit we are sinners (the Bible says all of us have sinned). Ten we have to ask Jesus to be our Savior. Jesus said no one comes to the Father (God) except through Him. that means that if anyone wants to go to Heaven, he has to accept Jesus as his Savior. I am ninety years old and I have loved Jesus for around eighty years. Why do I love Him? I love Jesus because He first loved me. He died on the cross for me. How could you not love someone who loves you that much. Jesus arose from the grave after three days, this is history. At the most, I probably have only a few years left on this earth, my body has run frail and I cannot walk without help. In Heaven, I will have a new body forever. My new body will be recognized as me in Heaven. When Jesus returned to earth after he was crucified, he was recognized. So, to get to heaven with your new body that will be recognized you have to make a choice. First you need to admit you are a sinner (the bible says we all sin) and then you need to be sorry that you sinned and then you need to accept Jesus as your savior. Jesus loves us all no matter what sin you have committed if you are truly sorry Jesus will forgive you. The truth about God is known to us instinctively. God has put this knowledge in our hearts. Since earliest time man has seen the earth and the sky and all god made and has known of his existence and great power. So there will no excuse when they stand before God at judgment day. He will punish sin wherever it is found. He will punish the heathen when they sin even though they never had god's written laws, because down in their hearts they know right from wrong. God's laws are written within them. Heaven is where God lives and, of course, Jesus, he is God's son. No one can get to Heaven if he hasn't accepted Jesus as their Savior. There will be no more death or mourning or agony or pain in Heaven. There will be no more death or suffering in Heaven. There will be no more tears in Heaven. Heaven will be a a perfect place. We love this earth even though it is not perfect. How much more will we love Heaven. Remember those who live immoral, who are idol worshipers, adulterers, or homosexuals will have no share in God's kingdom. Neither will thieves or greedy people, drunkards, slanderers will get to go to Heaven. But if you have made a choice to be sorry for your sine and turn from them and accept Jesus as your Savior, then you will inherit Heaven when you die. Jesus tells us in the bible that he is going to Heaven to prepare a place for us and in his Father's house are many mansions and He is preparing a place for us. My choice is an eternity with Jesus. The man is not a fool to give what he cannot keep to gain what he cannot lose. Remember he is just. The Lord despises those who say that bad is good and good is bad.

EPILOGUE

Would any sin on this earth be worth giving yourself to the Devil and spending your eternity in Hell? Would a sinful relationship be worth spending your eternity in Hell? An eternity does not end – it goes on and on and on.

We all sin and we know when we sin. If you are sorry for your sins and want Jesus to invite you to Heaven for your eternity, then just tell Jesus that you love him and you are sorry for your past sins. A lot of people think they can go to Heaven by just being good, but that is not true. You must be "born again". You must be sorry for your past sins and accept Jesus as your personal savior. That is all you need to do to spend your eternity in Heaven and if you are sorry for your past sins and call yourself a Christian, you belong to Christ, and when you die you can spend your eternity in Heaven.

Now get yourself a Bible.

Find yourself a loving church to belong to.

Just say "no" to sin and I'll see you in Heaven.

Printed in the United States
by Baker & Taylor Publisher Services